Bees and Honey

myth, folklore and traditions

by Luke Dixon

Northern Bee Books

BEES and HONEY, myth, folklore and traditions
© 2013 Luke Dixon

All rights reserved. No part of this publication may be reproduced, stored in a retrieval system, transmitted in any form or by any means electronic, mechanical, including photocopying, recording or otherwise without prior consent of the copyright holders.

ISBN 978-1-908904-30-0

Published by Northern Bee Books, 2013
Scout Bottom Farm
Mytholmroyd
Hebden Bridge
HX7 5JS (UK)

Design and artwork
D&P Design and Print
Worcestershire

Printed by Lightning Source, UK

Bees and Honey

myth, folklore and traditions

by Luke Dixon

'Pick up a bee from kindness and learn the limitations of kindness.'
Sufi proverb

BEES and HONEY myth, folklore and traditions

CONTENTS

INTRODUCTION 1

CREATION MYTHS 3

MAN, BEES AND HONEY 7

HOW THE BEES BECAME ORANGE 11

FOODS OF THE GODS 15

OF ARMS AND THE MAN, AND HONEY 25

SAINTS AND SINNERS 31

OF BEES AND BEEKEEPERS 35

CANDLES AND WAXEN IMAGES 39

BEES, THE FINAL FRONTIER 45

INDEX 51

'A bee was never caught in a shower.'
English proverb

INTRODUCTION

'Lick up the honey and ask no questions.'
Arabian proverb

A belief in the magic powers of bees affects us all. It may be a residual belief and we might not recognize it, but there it remains none the less. There will be few readers of this book who have not had someone light a candle on their birthday cake and made a wish as they blew it out, without so much as a thought as to where the potency of wax candles comes from. The most committed of secularists will go on a honeymoon after getting married, without thinking that the word refers to a month of fecundity stimulated by the eating of honey and the drinking of mead.

This book takes us from the beginning of time to the present day to show the ways in which bees and beekeeping, honey and wax, are a part of the culture, mythology, theology and folklore of every people in the world. And how humans and bees have had a magical relationship since the creation of the world itself.

We will spend a lot of time with the Ancient Greeks, journey through the harems of Arabia to the savannahs of Africa. And we will visit the English countryside too. Everywhere we go, across centuries and continents, we will find that the tiny humble honeybee, man's companion as long as there has been a man on the earth, has been and continues to be a source of wonder and magic.

BEES and HONEY myth, folklore and traditions

CREATION MYTHS

'Better a handful of bees than a basket full of flies.'
Moroccan proverb

In the beginning was the Bee. And the Mantis.
And the Bee flew over the waters that covered all of the world. Nowhere was there any land and so the Mantis had no place to rest. Knowing the Bee to be wise, Mantis went to her and said, 'There is no place for me to stand and eat, or to lay my head for sleep.'

The wise Bee took pity on the Mantis and said, 'Come with me and we will find a solid place for you to rest.'

The sun shone and with it came light. By the light of this sun Bee carried Mantis over the waters. Soon the sun grew tired and slept and the moon came to take her place in the sky. And so Bee and Mantis flew by the light of the moon until she became thin and died. Through the darkness flew Bee and Mantis till Bee could fly no further. 'It is cold and dark and I am tired,' said Bee. 'I must rest Mantis.' So down she sank, and as she sank the sun woke again and opened one eye. By the light of the sun, Bee saw below her a great white floating flower begin to open its arms to welcome the sun's first rays. Down flew Bee and laid Mantis in the heart of the flower. And Bee planted a seed within Mantis. And as the sun rose from his bed and warmed the white flower Mantis awoke, and from the seed left by the Bee was born the first of the San people.

The San people, the Bushmen of Southern Africa, have had a deep relationship with bees ever since and have harvested their honey from time immemorial.

There are other stories of bees and the creation of the world. Far away from the African savannah, the Slavic people tell of how the god Bielobog became bored with the endless expanse of water that he saw before him and decided to create Earth. Bielobog told his shadow self, Chernobog, to reach down below the waters and fetch up dirt. So Chernobog did as he was told and lifted dirt from below the water. Bielobog blessed the dirt and it became the land and with his blessing the land grew and became the Earth and the water became the Sea. The Earth continued to grow and Chernobog became jealous and wanted the Earth all to himself. He tried to push Bielobog into the sea and drown him. But though Bielobog was too powerful to be drowned he could not stop the Earth from growing. Only Chernobog, his shadow self, could do that but Chernobog would not tell Bielobog how it could be done. So Bielobog created the bee, a loyal and clever creature who could fly over land and water and spy on Chernobog. Bee went out to spy for her master and came back with news of what she had heard. All Bielobog need do was take two sticks and with them make a cross pointing in the four directions, north, south, east and west. Then he must say, 'Earth, you have grown enough, stop now and stay forever as you are.' The god Bielobog did as the bee had told him and the Earth stopped growing and was as we know it today. So grateful was the god Bielobog that he said to the bee that forever onwards nothing would be as sweet as that which came from her.

So it was that bees began to make honey in giant pots in the ground. And man found the honey and fed on it till he became fat and lazy. The gods of Brazil looked down on the people eating the honey from the homes of the bees and said, 'Man is becoming fat and lazy.' And the gods called the bees to them and said, 'You must leave the ground and live high in the trees, keeping your honey as far from man as you can.' This they did and ever since man has had to climb high to the hives of the bees to harvest their honey.

A tale from Thailand tells a different story of why the bees build their nests in the hollows of trees. Once upon a time elephants did not have trunks. One day a terrible fire swept through the forest where bees and the elephant lived. The bees feared they would die in the smoke and sought refuge in the mouth of the elephant.

The elephant did not want the bees in her mouth and trumpeted loudly to drive the bees out. But no matter how loudly she trumpeted the bees remained in the elephant's mouth. And the more the elephant trumpeted the more her face stretched until her nose became a trunk. Still the bees did not move. Finally the elephant breathed in the stinging smoke of the forest fire through her trunk and as soon as they smelt it the bees flew out of the elephant's mouth and into a hollow tree to escape the smoke. Bees have been escaping the smoke of forest fires ever since, and the wise beekeeper will smoke their colony to remind the bees of the fire in the forest and tell them to keep safe within the hive.

There was once a tale told in Bulgaria of how God created the earth and the sky, but he made the earth too big and so the sky did not fit over it. God was perplexed as to what to do. As he pondered the problem, he noticed the Devil and the hedgehog looking up at the sky and talking together. 'I wonder what they are saying,' he said to the bee, and the bee flew off to overhear their conversation. 'What a fool God is,' said the Devil to the hedgehog. 'Doesn't he realise that all he needs to do is hit the earth as hard as he can and then valleys and mountains will form and the sky will easily fit over it.' The bee returned and told God what the Devil had said and with a mighty thump God hit the earth, and mountains and valleys formed and the sky covered it completely. 'Thank you bee,' said God. 'I give you my blessing. May the honey you make be sacred and be used to mark births and marriages and even deaths. And may it have healing powers to cure the sick.'

In the Middle East stories were told of a god who created the world in six days. On the first day he created the light and the darkness; on the second day he divided the earth from the heavens; and on the third day he separated the earth from the sea and commanded the earth to bring forth grass, seed bearing herbs, and the fruit yielding trees. And the earth did as it was commanded. Next day God created the sun and the moon and the stars, and the seasons of the year. On the fifth day he populated the skies and the seas with life. Then came the sixth day. And God said, 'Let the earth bring forth living creatures of every kind.' So it was that every animal that now lives on earth was created. Seeing how good his creations were, God made one more creature. This one he made in his own image and called him 'man'. And God said that man could have dominion over the fish of the sea, and over the birds of the air, and over the cattle, and over all the earth, and over every creeping thing that crept on the earth. After six days spent creating the world God had a rest on the seventh. While God rested man looked around himself and saw the creatures that God had made and remembered the injunction to have dominion over them. And he saw the bees and he decided to become a keeper of them so as to please his God.

'I am come into my garden, my sister, my spouse:
I have gathered my myrrh with my spice;
I have eaten my honeycomb with my honey;
I have drunk my wine with my milk.
Eat, O friends; drink,
Yea, drink abundantly, O beloved.'
Song of Solomon

MAN, BEES AND HONEY

'He who holds the honey jar, gets to lick the fingers.'
Anatolian proverb

Once the bees had found their homes high up in hollow trees, they made honey in their combs of wax and had enough to feed themselves. There is a bird in Africa that leads people back to the bees' hidden hives and so lets them find honey to take home as a rare and precious food. The Honeyguide bird waits until man has taken the honey and then feeds on what is left behind. From Senegal in the west, across the Sahel to Ethiopia in the east, and south to the Cape and Table Mountain, is found The Greater Honeyguide, *Indicator indicator* and its small cousin *Indicator minor*, the Lesser Honeyguide. It has many names. The Xhosa call it Intakobusi, the Swazi Inhlava, the Tswana Tshetlho, the Tsonga Nhlalala, the Sotho of the south Molisa-linotši, and of the north Tshetlo. For the Zulu it is iNhlavebizelayo or uNomtsheketshe and for the Afrikaner Grootheuningwyser.

The Honeyguide birds are not being altruistic in leading humans to bees nests. For the bird is not able to open the beehive itself. It needs help. The help does not have to be human, a honey badger will do just as well. The Honeyguide bird will flutter around the badger or the human until they follow to the hive. Once there the greedy badger or human will break open the hive and take the honey. The bird will wait until all has quietened down and then fly down and eat up the larval bees that have been exposed and left behind.

It is a relationship that is as old as the bird, the bee, the badger and the Bushman, the oldest human on the planet. But it is a relationship that is disappearing as the Bushmen themselves disappear and those humans who replace them have no idea why the Honeyguide birds flutter around them as they drive across Africa in their 4x4s.

But the honey badger still understands what the Honeyguide birds are saying and will follow the birds not just to wild colonies of bees but also to the husbanded hives of human beekeepers and steal their honey too. The beekeepers of southern Africa have to take elaborate precautions to keep the badgers from their hives. What goes around comes around.

In Zimbabwe they tell how the Honeyguide bird was lonely and one day asked the bees to give him a wife. The bees said no and so the Honeyguide bird became angry and went off to tell man where the bees were living. When man heard he went and stole the bees' honey. Ever since in the lands of the San people, men climb high into the trees to harvest the wild honey.

In Afghanistan where the winters were hard, the bees had only enough honey to last them through the cold months when no flowers grew and there was no nectar to bring back to the hive. There was no honey to spare for the humans. The story goes that man took pity on the bees freezing in the snow, and said to them, 'I will make you homes of boxes of blue and of white and help you through the winter'. The bees were so pleased with their new homes that they made honey not just for themselves but with plenty to spare for the men who had built them their new homes.

Ever since the bees first flew out of the Elephant's mouth, bees and elephants have been very wary of each other. In Africa man hunted the wild animals around him. Tracking across the dry earth he moved in search of food and plants to eat. One day man said to himself, 'I am grown tired of running after my food and never having a home to call my own. I will build myself a home and cultivate the land around it, growing plants to feed myself. And I will keep animals tame around me for meat and milk to feed myself and for fur and hide to clothe myself.' Across southern Africa man built houses of wood and mud, and covered them with dried grass. The walls of the houses he painted white so they would reflect the rays of the sun and keep cool in the heat of the day.

Elephant continued to roam the countryside in search of food to eat. When she heard that man was growing plants to feed himself, the cunning Elephant said to herself, 'man is doing my work for me. Now I can relax. Instead of moving my big body across the savannah I can go and steal the food that man has grown.' As soon as man's tomatoes had ripened red in the sun, his potatoes were plump and juicy in the soil, and his maize gold on its tall stalks, Elephant tramped through the small fences surrounding the food and ate everything for herself. Man was very cross indeed and tried to scare Elephant away, but Elephant was too big and strong to be scared of a little man. The next year man grew his crops again, and again Elephant came and stole them all for herself. This time man tried to fight off Elephant with stick and stones, but Elephant's hide was too tough to feel the pricks and bumps of the sticks and stones and again she went away with her stomach full.

Then man remembered the bees and how they had once lived in the mouths of Elephant. Elephant had been afraid of the bees ever since and never went near a tree that had a hive of bees inside lest the bees came out of their tree and once more made their home in Elephant's mouth. So man went to the bees and made them an offer. He would build houses for the bees and look after them, just as he looked after the other animals that he kept for food. He would tend the bees, provide them food and water during the cold winters and keep them safe from fire. In return he asked for two things: a little honey from the hives if the bees could spare it, and protection from the marauding Elephant. 'We like your plan,' said the bees. We will come and live with you and you may take any honey we have to spare. If you look after us, we will protect your farm from the thieving Elephant, and scare her away when she comes in the night.'

As the next summer came to an end and man's crops were once again ready to be harvested, Elephant came crashing through the bush to take her fill. But as she reached the farm she stopped and stared. A cloud of bees was in the air, flying around a man-made box slung between two trees. Elephant stood very quietly and listened. Across the hot and hazy air came a sound that she had hoped never to hear again: the buzzing of a nest of bees. Elephant closed her mouth, wrapped up her trunk and turned around. 'Better to walk in search of food than have bees living in my mouth again', she thought.

So it was that man and bee began to live together. Now in Africa you can see the long boxes of bees that the farmers keep by their crops to frighten off the elephants.

' *I keep the bees and the bees keep me.*'
Friar Tuck, Robin Hood film 2010

HOW THE BEES BECAME ORANGE

'Bees have honey in their mouths, but stings in their tails.'
German proverb

The Ancient Greeks, in their myths, told of a time before even the Gods were born, when a race of Titans ruled, and where honey bees lived a secret life hidden in the deepest caves. Kronos was Lord of the Universe and greatest of the Titans. He came to power by overthrowing his father. Kronos mated with Rheia, another Titan, to give birth to the Gods of Olympus, immortals who could not be killed. But two other Titans, Gaia and Uranus, warned Kronos that he too would be overthrown by his son just as he had overthrown his father. So seriously did Kronos take this warning that every time his wife Rhea gave birth he took the child and swallowed it whole. Five times he did this – first to Hestia, then Demeter, Hera, Hades and Poseidon. Pregnant for a sixth time and fearful that Kronos would again take away her newborn child, Rheia asked advice of her parents who told her that she must travel to Lyktos in Crete and there hide the child as soon as she gave birth.

At Lyktos Rheia found a cave guarded by the Cretan gods, the Kouretes. There Rheia gave birth to Zeus and then returned to Kronos with a stone wrapped in swaddling clothes which she gave to Kronos and, thinking it to be the newborn child, this too he swallowed whole.

Before returning to Kronos, Rheia had given the baby up to the nymphs in the cave to look after and to the Kouretes to guard. In the cave lived the sacred bees. And nymphs. Nymphs, neither mortals nor immortals, ate the food of heaven, danced among the gods, and lived in the depths of the wonderful cave. It was the nymph Melissa who first discovered that the bees made honey in their comb. The other nymphs were so pleased, with what Melissa had found the little creature able to do, that they gave her name to the tiny insect and the honey it produced. The nymphs and bees lived in harmony inside the cave and Melissa taught the other nymphs how to harvest the honey and how to ferment it with water and make the golden drink of mead. There the sacred bees and the nymphs (who came to be known as the bee maidens or Melissae) feed the infant on honey, while the goat Amaltheia fed him on her milk. The Kouretes danced around the entrance of the cave and clashed together their shields and spears to make so much noise that it drowned the cries of the infant and also called the bees to defend it.

The child was named Zeus and so it was that, tended by the nymphs and fed on milk and honey, the baby Zeus grew into a god.

So grateful was Zeus for his diet of milk and honey, that he rewarded the bees by turning them to the colour of gold; the goat Amaltheia he transformed into a heavenly body and placed her high up in the sky where we may still see her today as the star Capella, the brightest star in the constellation Auriga, the charioteer, and the third brightest star in the northern hemisphere.

So secret was the hiding place of the young god that none were allowed to enter the cave. But the sweet smell of the honey that wafted from the cave's entrance was too enticing for all who smelt it to resist, and one day a group of young men dared venture into the cave to steal it. As they entered the cave they saw the young Zeus and as if by magic the joints of their armour split apart and the metal pieces fell noisily to the floor. Thinking it the warning sound of the Kouretes clashing their spears and shields, the sacred bees attacked the men, stung them and chased them from the cave. Ever since bees come flying when they hear the sound of metal crashing against metal. Even today beekeepers will 'tang' the bees when they need to catch a swarm, bashing pots and pans together. The bees remembering what happened to Zeus will come flying to the sound and in reward for their devotion the beekeeper will give them a new home.

For the San Bushmen honey was a prized food for themselves, their gods, and the spirits of the dead. To harvest the honey the Bushmen would use a bull-roarer (!goin !goin) which made a sound so loud that it caused the bees to swarm and leave the hive. Once the bees had left, the honey could be collected safely and taken home. In celebration, the women would sit in a circle and clap, while in the middle the men would dance the honey dance. As they danced through the night, the men were believed in some way to 'become' honey, and take on its magical potency. Only with the dawn would the dancing stop.

Ovid tells a different story of the tanging of the bees. A story of Dionysus, god of wine and ecstasy, the son of Zeus and Semele and the only god of the Greeks to have a mortal parent. Dionysus's companions, the satyrs, enjoyed nothing more than making music, drinking wine and cavorting with women. One day they were making so much noise with the clanging of their cymbals that swarms of bees appeared and followed the noise. Dionysus collected the bees and found them a home in a hollow tree. Visiting the bees the next day Dionysus found that they had made honey. Sometime later an old man named Silenus came upon Dionysus and the satyrs eating honey. Once he had tasted this wonderful new food Silenus plotted to take some for himself, but the satyrs would not tell him where the bees were living. Silenus went off on his donkey looking for the bees and soon found them by the buzzing sounds they were making. But the bees did not want their honey stolen and chased and stung the old man who fell off his donkey and called for help. The satyrs heard him and laughed aloud. Dionysus laughed too but soothed the old man's stings with mud. That is the story of how Dionysus discovered honey and why it was that the Greeks offered honey-cakes to the God in thanks.

Once Zeus had grown to manhood, fed on milk and honey, he returned to Othrys, confronted his father Kronos and forced him to vomit up the siblings that he had swallowed. First out of the Titan's stomach came the stone which Rheia had wrapped in swaddling clothes. This Zeus placed on earth at Delphi where mortals beheld it in wonder for centuries. Then came the other gods, Zeus's brothers and sisters – Poseidon, last to be swallowed, then Hades, Hera, Demeter and last of all Hestia. And so began a mighty war between the generations – between the Titans from their home on Mount Othrys and the Gods led by Zeus on their home on Mount Olympus. It was a war that neither Gods nor Titans could win so equal were their strengths.

(The stone would be kept at the temple of Zeus's son Apollo. The temple itself was made of wax from bees and feathers from birds after the Oracle commanded: 'Bring together feathers ye birds and wax ye bees.')

Zeus asked his mother Gaia for advice as to how the war could be won. She told him he must free the fearsome one-eyed Cyclopes and the Hundred-Handers from the depths of the earth. This Zeus did. Then he went to his friends the bees who had raised him from childhood and asked them for the honey which they had fed him on as a child. The bees gathered together all the honey from their combs deep in the Cretan caves and Zeus fed it to the Hundred-Handers and the Cyclopes. So strong did these monsters become on this magical food that they were ready to go into battle for Zeus and overthrow the Titans.

The Cyclopes forged thunder and lightning as weapons. The Hundred-Handers threw great rocks, three hundred at a time. Thus it was that the Titans were defeated and Zeus dethroned his father as had been prophesied, and so became the greatest of all the gods.

The gods lived on Olympus from where they ruled the Universe. Ichor ran through their veins and they fed on nectar and ambrosia – foods of the gods.

'The men of experiment are like the ant; they only collect and use. But the bee gathers its materials from the flowers of the garden and of the field, and transforms and digests it by a power of its own.'
Leonardo da Vinci

FOODS OF THE GODS

'Is Honey really magic?' Serena asked. She is a very attractive young married friend of mine, who is keenly interested in health.
'I think it is,' I replied, 'and I believe that everyone who has ever studied the history of Honey is convinced that it has in it a magic ingredient.'
'How exciting,' Serena exclaimed.
'In Honey there is contained, I am convinced, the Elixir of Life. This is the reason why honey is stimulating to sex, and it is also responsible for its fantastic healing properties.'
'Tell me more about Honey,' Serena begged. 'I really know very little about it.'
Dame Barbara Cartland, The Magic of Honey

The gods of the Ancient Greeks lived on the top of Mount Olympus, feeding on nectar and ambrosia. Today we do not know for certain what these foods were. They were produced by the bees and taken to the gods by winged doves. Ambrosia was eaten and nectar drunk, so most likely they were different forms of honey, set and liquid, or honey in its comb and honey extracted and ready to be drunk. For the African Bushmen, one of the potent magical qualities of honey is that it is a substance that can be both eaten and drunk.

Ambrosia was a food so wondrous that it could make a man immortal.

Zeus had a daughter with his sister Demeter, the beautiful Persephone. So beautiful was she that Zeus's brother Hades lusted after her and wanted her for his own. Hades told Zeus of his desire and together they created a trap for the girl. While Persephone was gathering flowers in a meadow, she was led away from her companions by the sight of a hundred-flowered narcissus. As she reached out to the flower, put there by her father, the earth beneath her opened up and her uncle Hades emerged from the underworld on his chariot and abducted her down into the earth to be his consort. Hearing her screams Demeter rushed to her daughter but arrived too late. Persephone had disappeared.

Demeter did not eat or drink for nine days and nine nights but wandered in search of her daughter. Then, meeting up with the goddess Hecate, she went to Helios the sun god for advice. 'You see everything as you travel across the sky each day,' she told him. 'Did you see what happened to my daughter?'

'Hades has captured Persephone,' he told her, 'and taken her down to the Underworld to be his bride.' In her anger at what she had been told, Demeter left Olympus to live amongst the mortals.

Disguised as an old woman, Demeter was taken in by the daughters of King Keleos and their mother, Queen Metaneira, who offered Demeter the job of nursemaid to her new born son Demophon. So grateful was Demeter and so loving of her infant charge, that she decided to make the baby immortal. Every night she burnt away a little of the child's mortal flesh and anointed the wound with ambrosia. So bit by bit, burn by burn, she replaced Demophon's mortal flesh with immortality. (Thetis, another goddess, tried the same trick with her mortal son Achilles but as she anointed him with ambrosia, forgot the heel by which she was holding him and Achilles' heel became the weak spot which led to his death.)

Eventually Demeter had Persphone returned to her, but at a price. She was forced to spend four months of every year with Hades in the underworld, and during those months no crops would grow on earth and no flowers would bloom. So it was that the bees became even busier making honey whenever they could and storing up their magical, life-giving food through the bleak winter months.

Ambrosia was strictly for the gods. On his journey to Hades, Odysseus saw Tantalus, condemned forever to the underworld for stealing nectar and ambrosia from the gods. He suffered a 'tantalising' torment ever since, standing up to his neck in water, racked by thirst but unable to drink the water which receded every time he bent his head.

The love between God and mortal has been fraught with difficulties. The goddess Eos fell in love with a mortal, the beautiful boy Tithonos. Eos asked Zeus to give her lover eternal life and Zeus did exactly as was asked of him. But while he gave the boy eternal life he did not give him eternal youth. As Tithonos grew old, grey and infirm, Eos fed him with ambrosia in a desperate attempt to make him young again.

Ambrosia had many uses. The Goddess Hera, Zeus's sister, used it to it to cleanse all defilement from her lovely flesh before seducing her brother Zeus, bathing in milk, pouring soft oils on her body, and showering in ambrosia before going to Mount Olympus.

From the time of the Ancient Greeks, mortals have believed in the healing and life giving properties of honey. Every since it has been used to treat burns, anoint deities, cure sickness, as an aphrodisiac, as a means to fend off death and as a way to welcome life. From the Scottish Highlands to Ancient Babylonia, from Finland to Greece, amongst Christians, Muslims, Hindus and Jews, there are traditions of smearing the lips of new born babies with a drop of honey, a sacred substance, as a first food.

In Hindu mythology there are close links between gods and honey. In Sanskrit the word for honey is 'madhu'. The gods Vishnu, Krishna and Indra were called Madhava – the nectar born ones - and Kama, the Hindu god of love, carries a bow strung with bees as a symbol of the pain and sweetness that love can bring. Kundalini, the life force, lies coiled like a snake at the base of the spine in the muladhara chakra. A residual power of pure desire, the sound of its uncoiling is said to be like that of a swarm of bees.

In Hindu mythology amrita is a honey-like elixir, much like ambrosia in Greek mythology. During the 'deluge', the amrita became lost in the cosmic ocean of milk. Gods and devils joined together to save the precious amrita by churning the milky ocean. As they churned the milk sacred beings were created - the goddess of wine and the goddess of beauty, the moon and the cow, until at last the physician of the gods emerged with a bowl containing the lost amrita.

Honey and milk are mixed together to make madhu-parka as an offering to the Hindu gods. When a Hindu child enters the world, jatakarma is performed to welcome the child into the family, by putting some honey in the child's mouth and whispering the name of God in the child's ear.

Ayurvedic medicine sets great store by the medicinal properties of honey and it is called by many names. Madhu of course, but also *makshika, madwikam, kshaudram, saradham, vantham, varadi, bringavantham* and *pushparasolbhavam*. The classic Ayuvedic text, 'Ashtanga Hridaya', lists eight different types of honey each with its special uses. The quality of a honey can be judged by the way in which it pours. The very best honey will drop down in the shape of a serpent, coiling like Kundalini.

In the Norse myths, it is mead that is renowned for its magic powers. When the all-wise God Kvasir was killed by the Dwarves, they made mead from a mixture of his blood and honey, which they kept in the cauldron called Othrörir. Suttung the giant took the cauldron off to his mountain home for safe keeping where his daughter Gunloth kept guard over it. The great god Odin had a desire to taste of the blood-red mead and disguised himself as a serpent to enter Suttung's lair in secret. There he made love to Gunloth and with her help drank down the mead in three mighty gulps from the cauldron. Then deserting the giant's daughter, he transformed himself into an eagle and flew home to Valhalla.

The eating of honey is central to the observance of the Jewish New Year. Apples are dipped in honey, cake is made from honey, challah loaves are eaten with honey, and dumplings are cooked in honey, all in the hope of a 'sweet' new year. But is it kosher? Jewish dietary laws prohibit the eating of some animals and the products derived from them, including insects: 'And every creeping thing that flieth is unclean unto you: they shall not be eaten,' commands the Bible. So the bee is a non-kosher animal and yet the honey that bees produce is regarded as kosher and has been since the time of the Jewish patriarch Jacob. It was once believed that bees merely collected honey and did not make it, a belief almost certainly current in Old Testament times. So honey was kosher. Now that we know that bees do actually produce honey, the kosher paradox is resolved by distinguishing the 'honey' stomach in which the nectar is carried from the bees 'real' stomach which is a true part of her digestive system.

The first mention of honey in the Bible is as one of the gifts sent by Jacob to his sons when they went down to Egypt to seek food during the famine. When Moses first hears the voice of God at the burning bush, the voice tells him:

'I have surely seen the affliction of my people which are in Egypt, and have heard their cry by reason of their taskmasters; for I know their sorrows; And I am come down to deliver them out of the hand of the Egyptians, and to bring them up out of that land unto a good land and a large, unto a land flowing with milk and honey.'

Throughout the world honey is thought of as an aphrodisiac and linked with fertility. To ensure a successful marriage, a Polish bride was blindfolded before her wedding and honey smeared on her lips. In Bengal, the Brahmans smeared the honey on the pudenda of a bride to be. And a honeymoon today is a reminder that honey and mead were eaten and drunk in the month after marriage to ensure the fertility of the bride and groom.

There are stories of the magical effects of honey in the Arab world. In his fifteenth century manual of eroticism 'The Perfumed Garden', the Arab Sheik Muhammad ibn Muhammad al-Nafzawi gives many examples of the uses of honey, from preventing premature ejaculation to 'increasing the dimensions of small members and for making them splendid'. Sir Richard Burton, Victorian adventurer and Arabist, translated the work into English.

One chapter ' treats of the size of the virile member.' 'This,' we are told, 'is of the first importance both for men and women. For the men because from a good-sized and vigorous member there springs the affection and love of women; for the women, because it is by such members that their amorous passions are appeased, and the greatest pleasure is procured for them. This is evident from the fact that many men, solely by reason of their insignificant members, are, as far as coition is concerned, objects of aversion to women, who likewise entertain the same sentiment with regard to those whose members are soft, nerveless, and relaxed. Their whole happiness consists in the use of robust and strong members.'

The Shiek and Burton have two top tips for using honey to make the member bigger:

'A man, therefore, with a small member, who wants to make it grand or fortify it for the coitus, must rub it before copulation with tepid water, until it gets red and extended by the blood flowing into it, in consequence of the heat; he must then anoint it with a mixture of honey and ginger, rubbing it in sedulously. Then let him join the woman; he will procure for her such pleasure that she objects to him getting off her again.

'Another remedy consists in a compound made of a moderate quantity of pepper, lavender, galanga, and musk, reduced to powder, sifted, and mixed up with honey and preserved ginger. The member after having been first washed in warm water, is then vigorously rubbed with the mixture; it will then grow large and brawny, and afford to the woman a marvellous feeling of voluptuousness.'

'The efficacy of all these remedies is well known,' says the author, 'and I have tested them.'

'The Perfumed Garden' climaxes with of a story of the deeds of three men, Abou el Heïloukli, Abou el Heïdja and Mimoun, 'who have been justly praised, and whose history is truly marvellous.' Here is how Burton retells it:

The brothers Abou el Heïdja and Abou el Heïloukh and their negro servant Mimoun come to the secret harem of the lovely Princess Zohra with whom Abou el Heïdja is in love. Zohra thought to herself, 'It is only by a stratagem I can get rid of these men,' and decides, 'to set them tasks which they will be unable to accomplish as conditions for my consent.'

'Abou el Heïdja,' she said to him, 'As regards you, I impose upon you the task of deflowering eighty virgins without ejaculating. Such is my will!'

'Abou el Heïloukh, what I require of you is to remain here, in the presence of these women and virgins, for fifty consecutive days with your member during this period always in erection during day and night.'

'Mimoun,' she said pointing a woman called Mouna who was insatiable as regards coition, 'your task shall be, to do this woman's business without resting for fifty consecutive days; you need not ejaculate unless you like; but if the excess of fatigue forces you to stop, you will not have fulfilled your obligations.'

Each accepted the challenge given them asking only for drink as sustanance. Abou el Heïdja asked for camel's milk mixed with honey; Abou el Heïloukh demanded the juice pressed out of pounded onions mixed with honey; and Mimoun, on his part, asked for yolks of eggs and bread.

So it was that with the aid of their honeyed drinks the brothers Abou succeeded in the tasks set them by Princess Zohra. Only Mimoun began to tire and on hearing this Abou el Heïdja cried, 'In the name of God! if he does not carry out his task, aye, and if he does not go beyond it for ten days longer, he shall die the vilest of deaths!'

So it was that his zealous servant never during the period of fifty days took any rest in his work of copulation, and kept going on, besides, for ten days longer, as ordered by his master.

Mouna, on her part, had the greatest satisfaction, as this feat had at last appeased her ardour for coition. Mimoun, having remained victor, could then take his seat with his companions.

Then said Abou el Heïdja to Zohra. 'See, we have fulfilled all the conditions you have imposed upon us. It is now for you to accord me the favours which, according to our agreement, were to be the price if we succeeded.' 'It is but too true!' answered the princess, and she gave herself up to him, and he found her excelling the most excellent. As to the negro, Mimoun, he married Mouna. Abou el Heïloukh chose, amongst all the virgins, the one whom he had found most attractive.

They all remained in the palace, giving themselves up to good cheer and all possible pleasures, until death put an end to their happy existence and dissolved their union.

For those who might want to try out the honey remedy, 'The Perfumed Garden' ends with a recipe:

'Take one part of the juice pressed out of pounded onions, and mix it with two parts of purified honey. Heat the mixture over a fire until the onion juice has disappeared and the honey only remains. Then take the residue from the fire, let it get cool, and preserve it for use when wanted. Then mix of the same one *aoukia* with three *aouak* of water, and let chick-peas be macerated in this fluid for one day and one night.

'This beverage is to be partaken of during winter and on going to bed. Only a small quantity is to be taken, and only for one day. The member of him who has drunk of it will not give him much rest during the night that follows. As to the man who partakes of it for several consecutive days, he will constantly have his member rigid and upright without intermission. A man with an ardent temperament ought not to make use of it, as it may give him a fever. Nor should the medicine be used three days in succession except by old or cold-tempered men. And lastly, it should not be resorted to in summer.'

Unlike Burton and the Sheik this author cannot vouch for the efficacy of this remedy for he has not tested it.

While Sir Richard Burton was translating 'The Perfumed Garden', his wife Isabel was translating a novel by the Brazilian writer José de Alencar. This was 'Iracema' - Honey Lips - and tells of how the Brazilian race was born through Moacir, son of the native Brazilian princess Iracema and the European Martim, a perfect marriage of the natural innocence and beauty of the honey-lipped Iracema and the culture and knowledge of the colonial immigrant Martim. Out of this marriage a new Brazilian race was born. The story has the flavour of the myths of the Greeks:

'Far, very far from that Sierra which purples the horizon, was born Iracema. Iracema, the virgin with the honey lips, whose hair, hanging below her palm-like waist, was jet black as the wing of the Graiina bird. The comb of the little Jaty-bee which makes delicious honey was less sweet than her smile, and her breath excelled the perfume exhaled by the vanilla of the woods'.

Bee-stings have long been thought to prevent or cure rheumatism. There are people today who will have themselves stung by bees in order to ward off arthritis. Like many of the honey related remedies, evidence for their efficacy is largely anecdotal. But there is now some scientific research into bee stings and arthritis and some clinical evidence to show that bee venom can control the harmful inflammation in joints that leads to rheumatoid arthritis through the production of increased levels of anti-inflammatory hormones called glucocorticoids.

The beekeepers of New Zealand believe that they produce the very best honey in the world, infused with the health giving properties that come from the nectar of the Manuka plant. No other honey, save Sidr Honey from the Hadramaut Mountains in Arabia, commands as great a price, and it is sought for across the world. The Manuka plant is native to Australia and was taken to New Zealand by Polynesian seafarers. Neither country had the honeybee until European settlers introduced it. An evergreen shrub with little white flowers and its Maori name, the Manuka was known as the tea tree by Captain Cook who sailors used it to make a palatable brew in the absence of the real thing. Those who sell Manuka honey claim it 'to have some very special properties indeed,' though they do not say whether it can bestow immortality on those who feed on it or use it to anoint their skin.

The healing powers of honey were once believed to extend even beyond death. Honey was used by the Egyptians, Babylonians, Persians, Assyrians and Arabs to preserve the corpses of kings and emperors so that their bodies survived even human mortality. Alexander the Great was famously preserved in honey. King Herod, who ordered the killing of every infant in Judea, was not only jealous of the baby Jesus. Jealous also of his beautiful wife, Marianne, her ordered her to be executed. But his love survived her death, and even though he had had her killed and kept her dead body preserved in honey for seven years so as to love her beyond the grave.

In China they talk of the rarest of sweetmeats, a confection so wonderous that it can bestow healing properties greater than any medicine. It is known as Mellified Man, and even today, if you know where to ask, it is said that you can find street pharmacists who will sell you it at a price. Its rarity is easily understood when you know how it is made. Nearing the end of their lives, men would offer their bodies for mummification. But unlike the embalming of the bodies of Alexander and Marianne, this process began *before* death. The men would eat a diet only of honey. Nothing else would pass their lips. Slowly they would die a death by honey and the mellified men would be put in stone coffins and their bodies submerged in yet more honey. A hundred years would pass before the mellified man was ready to be eaten, sold in small pieces as the ultimate cure-all.

'Honey is a wonderful substance but it does not help the dead.'
Persian proverb

OF ARMS AND THE MAN, AND HONEY

'A drop of honey will not sweeten the ocean.'
Greek proverb

Odysseus was the warrior that came up with the plan of the Trojan Horse - a wooden horse full of soldiers that was dragged into the besieged city of Troy by its citizens leading to their defeat when the soldiers emerged. That defeat ended the long Trojan wars.

Odysseus' epic voyage home from the wars was told by Homer in his poem 'The Odyssey'. Honey plays a recurring role in the story. Early on the journey Odysseus is given a gift of twelve jars of wine sweetened with honey by a grateful Maron, priest of Apollo whose life Odysseus has spared. On reaching Sicily the crew rest in a cave full of sheep, goats, milk and cheese.

The cave is the store room of Polyphemos, a Cyclops, or one-eyed giant. When Polyphemos comes home with his sheep and goats at the end of the day he finds Odysseus and his soldiers in his cave and in a greedy rage snatches up two of the men and gobbles them down whole before rolling a great boulder across the caves entrance and trapping the others.

In the morning Polyphemos has two more of Odysseus's men for breakfast, replaces the boulder and goes off for the day. 'Your men are tasty,' Polyphemos tells Odysseus before he leaves, 'and I will eat them all. You must be the tastiest of them all so I will save you till last.'

Knowing he has not the strength to kill the giant, Odysseus comes up with a plan. When Polyphemos returns to the cave at the end of the day he asks Odysseus his name. 'My name is nobody,' replies Odysseus as Polphemos eats another two of his men. Odysseus offers the Cyclops the honey-sweetened wine that was a gift from Maron to wash down his human food. Greedy as ever Polyphemos quickly guzzles down all the wine and falls into a drunken stupor. As soon as he is asleep Odysseus takes a stake he has sharpened during the day and plunges it deep into the Cyclop's single eye. Polyphemos wakes screaming with pain. Hearing his cries in the dark the other Cyclopes come to help him but when they ask what is happening Polyphemos tells them that 'No-one' is trying to kill him. Laughing they walk away.

Next morning the blinded Polyphemos moves the boulder from the cave entrance and lets his sheep out one by one, stroking each to make sure it is not a man that he is letting out of the cave. But Odysseus and his men are clinging to the undersides of the sheep and so escape. Safely back on board his ship Odysseus calls out to the Cyclops, 'I am not No-one, I am Odysseus,' and sails away across the sea.

Polyphemos will have his revenge for his father is Poseidon, God of the Sea and brother to Zeus mightiest of the Gods.

Honey plays an important part in Odysseus's adventures on his long voyage home. On the island of Aiaia the enchantress Circe transforms his men into pigs by hiding her magic potion in honey-laced wine. Before his journey to Hades, Odysseus makes an offering of milk and honey to the Gods of the underworld. There he meets the shade of Teiresias who prophesies that Poseidon is so angry with what Odysseus has done to his son Polyphemos the Cyclops that he will make his journey home a hard one. And so it proves.

Homer tells of the wondrous caves of Ithaca where the Nereids made their divine webs of purple laced with gold and where the clustering bees attended their waxen works and built their combs of honey from the ceiling. It was from the mouth of the cave that the great mighty Zeus, god of the sky and ruler of Olympus came to meet Poseidon, god of the seas and father to Polyphemos. Poseidon asks that he might torment Odyssseus for what he has done to his son and Zeus agrees.

Leaving Hades they encounter the Sirens whose singing enchants all men. Heeding Circe's warning Odysseus stops up the ears of his crew with beeswax so they cannot hear the Siren song.

It took Odysseus ten years to make the voyage back to Ithica. All the while his wife Penelope had remained faithful and wept daily at her husband's absence. On her Odysseus' return the goddess Athena sent Penelope off into a sweet slumber laying her down on her couch until her limbs became heavy with sleep. Then the goddess 'shed grace and beauty over her and washed her face with the ambrosial loveliness that Venus wears when she goes dancing with the Graces; she made her taller and of a more commanding figure, while as for her complexion it was whiter than sawn ivory.' The years fell away and Penelope awoke as beautiful as she had been the day Odysseus left her.

Another poet, Virgil in his epic poem 'The Aeniad', tells the story of Aeneas, founder of Rome.

Zeus was responsible for the conception of Aeneas by forcing the goddess Aphrodite to make love to a mortal, the Trojan Prince Anchises. Aeneas, like Zeus, was raised by nymphs, in a cave on Mount Ida.

While Odysseus is journeying the seas returning from the Trojan wars, Aeneas is voyaging to Italy. On his way he and his men see the Cyclops Polyphemos, just blinded by Odysseus, wading into the sea to wash the blood from his wounded eye socket.

In telling his tale of arms and the man, of the life of Aeneas, his wars in Latinum and his founding of Rome, Virgil laces his epic poem with stories and imagery of bees and beekeeping. He likens the builders of Carthage to bees in spring:

'Such is their toil, and such their busy pains,
As exercise the bees in flow'ry plains,
When winter past, and summer scarce begun,
Invites them forth to labor in the sun;
Some lead their youth abroad, while some condense
Their liquid store, and some in cells dispense;
Some at the gate stand ready to receive
The golden burthen, and their friends relieve;
All with united force, combine to drive
The lazy drones from the laborious hive:
With envy stung, they view each other's deeds;
The fragrant work with diligence proceeds.'

And Virgil likens the Italians, defending their city from Aeneas, to bees defending a hive from smoke:

'As, when the swain, within a hollow rock,
Invades the bees with suffocating smoke,
They run around, or labor on their wings,
Disus'd to flight, and shoot their sleepy stings;
To shun the bitter fumes in vain they try;
Black vapors, issuing from the vent, involve the sky.'

Aeneas wins this battle with the Latins and soon Rome will stand where he is victorious.

Virgil's weaving of bees and hives into his epic poem will be familiar to a beekeeper today, some two millenia after it was written. No surprise, for Virgil was himself a beekeeper. One story of Virgil and his beekeeping tells of some soldiers who raided the poet's home and tried to steal his belongings. His servants grabbed hold of all they could and hid everything amongst the beehives, then opened the hives and let the bees swarm around the soldiers who quickly took flight. Once they had gone Virgil and his servants quietly closed up the hives and the bees quickly returned home. All was soon quiet again and the robbers never returned.

This is not the only story of bees being used for protection against theft. In this one they protect themsleves against theft. In this St. Medard is patron saint of the weather and protector of those, like beekeepers, who work in the open air. He is also the saint to pray to if you have toothache. Medard was Bishop of Vermand in Picardy, and a beekeeper. A thief stole his hive of bees one night but the bees escaped, stinging and chasing the thief back to the abbey and making him fall down and plead for forgiveness from the Bishop. As Medard stretched out his hand in benediction, the bees left off stinging the thief and flew back to their hive.

How the Bee got her Sting

One day the queen of the hive brought honey herself to Mount Olympus to give to Zeus who she had known since he was a baby. Zeus was so grateful for the gift that he promised the bee whatever she desired. 'Give me, I pray thee, a sting, ' she asked,' so that if any mortal tries to take my honey I can kill him.'
But Zeus loved the mortals so thought before he answered the bee's request. At last he said, 'I have made you a promise, and I must keep to it. You shall have your sting. But if you use it, the sting will remain in the mortal, tearing your body in two, and it is you that will die.'
The moral of this fable is that:
Evil wishes, like chickens, come home to roost.
Aesop

SAINTS AND SINNERS

'The buzzing of the flies does not turn them into bees.'
Georgian proverb

Beekeeping now flourishes in Ireland. It was not always so. Centuries ago the island of Ireland was infested by snakes, but had no bees at all. It was Saint Patrick who drove the snakes from Ireland, and it was Saint Modomnoc who brought the bees there.

St. David, patron saint of Wales, kept bees. In his life of St. David, the Welsh poet Rhygyvarch mentions the story of Saint Modomnoc and the bees of Ireland. Modomnoc was a monk at the monastery where St. David's cathedral now stands. Of all the monks who tended the hives at the monastery, Modomnoc was the best of the beekeepers and the one most beloved by the bees. But the monk was an Irishman and longed to return to the land of his fathers.

The time came for the other monks bid him farewell as Modomnoc stepped aboard ship to begin the journey home. As soon as the ship set sail, the bees sensed the monk's departure and flew after him, clustering on the ship's prow. Modomnoc did not want to defraud the other monks of the bees that were rightfully theirs and so had the ship turn around and came back to the monastery. The bees flew after him and returned to their hives. David blessed him and once more Modomnoc set off and once more the bees followed him and once more the monk returned. Three times this happened. On the third occasion David said to Modomnoc that he must leave and let the bees go with him. So David blessed Modomnoc and the bees, saying, 'May the land to which you go abound with your offspring. May your progeny never be wanting in it. Our monastery will be deserted forever by you. Never shall your offspring grow up in it.'

So it was, Rhygyvarch tells us, that Ireland became enriched with an abundance of honey. And that is why, the poet says, that all attempts since to keep bees in St. David's have failed and any swarms brought to the city, 'remain there but a little while and then cease.'

Modomnoc is now patron saint of bees, though not of beekeepers. Bees and beekeepers have other patron saints as well, though the reasons for the links between these saints and bees remain obscure. Saint Ambrose of Milan was known as the Honey Tongued Doctor so powerful was his preaching. Bees and beehives have become associated with him and he is also the patron of chandlers, wax refiners and other trades dependent on the bee. Saint Bernard of Clarivaux, another patron of bees and beekeepers was known as the Mellifluous Doctor of the Church. In Christian iconography the bee has associations of wisdom which may be why Saint Dominic de Guzman and Saint Isidore of Seville are often represented with swarms of bees around them.

Only one saint is patron to the keepers of bees and not bees themselves: Saint Valentine. It is unclear why Valentine should be linked to beekeepers, but it may be through the Roman feast of Lupercalia which Saint Valentine's Day replaced. Lupercalia was a feast day of purification, health and fertility. Plutarch writes that on this day, February 14th, 'many of the noble youths run up and down through the city naked, for sport and laughter striking those they meet with stinging thongs. And many women deliberately get in their way, holding out their hands to be struck, believing that the pregnant will thus be helped in delivery, and the barren to pregnancy.'

There is even a miracle associated with bees, brought about by the Irish beekeeping Saint Gobnat. One version tells how she was interrupted while at her bee hives by a chieftain named O'Hierley who asked for help to recover his stolen cattle. Gobnat agreed to help the chieftain on the condition that he converted to Christianity. This seemed a small price to pay for the return of his valuable cattle so O'Hierley readily agreed. With a prayer and the sign of the cross, Gobnat transformed one of her hives into a brass helmet for the chieftain, and the bees into a troop of soldiers ready to do battle on his behalf. Some say the helmet is still to be seen, converted into a bell to call the faithful to worship.

Another telling of the story also involves the chieftain O'Hierley but this time he and his soliders are battling not cattle rustlers but another clan. It is a prayer from O'Hierley that Saint Gobnat answers and again a hive of straw is turned into a helmet of brass, and a swarm of bees into a disciplined army of soldiers. There are those who say that the helmet is still kept in the O'Hierley family, not as a bell but as a font. A drop of water from the font given to a dying man will guarantee his place in heaven.

It was not a saint who brought bees to America but the first English settlers. They also brought legends and traditions with them. The Native Americans called the new insect 'the white man's fly', for they had not seen the honeybee before the settlers brought their hives on the long and dangerous journey across the Atlantic. The Cherokee are not the only tribe to have stories of the bee, though their tales must be post-Colombian. The Cherokee myth tells not of bees arriving on the white man's boat, but goes back to a time when men could still talk with the animals, and hold conversations with the Creator God.

One day man asked the Creator God for something sweet to eat and so the Creator created the bee. The bee made for herself a home in the hollow of a tree and there she made her sweet tasting honey. When people came and asked for honey, the bee gave enough for everybody. But man was greedy and as soon as he had he eaten the honey that bee had given him, he came back for more. 'I have no more honey to give you,' said the bee, 'for you have eaten it all.'

So man went back to the Creator God and asked more honey. This time God asked the flower people to spread flowers across the land, blooms of every colour rich with pollen and nectar. And when the flowers bloomed, God made more bees to pollinate them and use their nectar to make honey. The bees had to keep enough honey to feed their young, but the rest they gave to man. But still man wanted more, for now he had developed a taste for sweetness that could not easily be satisfied. 'We must keep what honey we have to feed our new born,' said the bees. 'If you want more you will have to wait.'

This time man went to the flower people and asked them to make more flowers so that the bees might make more honey. 'You must wait till spring,' the flower people said. But man was greedy and would not wait till the spring. Instead he returned to the hive, stole the last of the honey and killed many of the bees as he did so. The bees that survived were angry and afraid and asked the Creator what they should do.

The Creator too was angry at the greed of man. He called to the flower people and told them to make briar bushes and have them grow all around the hive. Then he told the bees to feed on the briars. So the bees ate the briars and their thorns became the bees stings.

When man returned to steal more honey he found a patch of briars all around the hive. His greed was so strong that he cut through the briars and, covered in scratches, reached the hive. When the bees heard man outside the hive, the swarmed out and stung him until he was forced to run away in pain.

From that day on man has treated flowers and plants and bees with great respect and learnt to curb his greed. Now he takes from nature only what he needs and helps replace what he harvests.

We now know that bees do not see the colours that we do. They cannot detect red. But while they cannot see the bottom end of the spectrum that humans can see, they can see past the top end of that spectrum to ultra-violet, and can see colours that we do not even have names for. Maybe that explains the common story found in central Europe of how the bee ignored God's injunction to rest on the seventh day but continued to collect nectar especially from the Red Clover which was the most abundant of flowers. So angry was God at being disobeyed that he punished them with the words, 'Never again will you find honey in the flowers of the Red Clover.'

'The fruit of bees is desired by all, and is equally sweet to kings and beggars and it is not only pleasing but profitable and healthful; it sweetens their mouths, cures their wounds, and conveys remedies to inward ulcers.'
Saint Ambrose

OF BEES AND BEEKEEPERS

'The bee stays not in a hive that has no honey.'
Turkish proverb

Men and bees have spoken to each other since time began. Today a beekeeper will put their ear to the hive to listen to the bees during the winter months, and when the hive is open in the summer, the sounds that the bees make will tell the beekeeper whether they are happy to be disturbed and when it is time to close up the hive.

It is a universal custom, across time, geography and culture, to tell the bees of important moments in the lives of the humans around them. Most importantly of all, bees must be told of a death, especially if it is the death of their keeper, and this tradition is still strong amongst beekeepers around the world. Some will drape black crêpe on the hive, put a black ribbon around it, or place a portion of the funeral food near the hive entrance. Some will turn the hive away from the funeral procession as it passes, or even move the hive away completely. Always the news will be told to the bees in a gentle whisper, just as a beekeeper will always work gently and quietly when opening a hive. There are some who say that if the bees are not told of the death of their keeper they will fly off in search of them, just as Modomnoc's bees flew after him to Ireland.

The invocation in Switzerland is: 'Abeilles, petites abeilles, je viens vous aventir que votre maître est mort – bees, little bees, I have come to tell you that your master is dead.'

Some tap on the hive first with the key of the house before saying anything. The beekeepers of Japan, who do not use smoke to calm their bees, always tap on their hives to calm the bees and drive them down before opening them. In Lithuania if someone close to the bees dies, a bunch of keys is rattled in front of the beehive, or the bees too will die.

Such superstitions go back to antiquity. John Molle, in his 'Living Librarie' of 1621, tells that, 'if the mistress of a house dies and the bees are not removed or turned over [faced in a different direction], they will die in their hives.' Four hundred years later, there was a report from Allentown, Pennsylvania, of a man giving orders 'to have his beehives moved from their places at the death of his daughter, when the procession started from the house, to prevent the death of another member of the family, several others suffering at the same time with the same disease which caused the daughter's death.'

Although telling the bees of death seems a universal custom, many cultures tell of births and marriages as well as deaths, and some will decorate their hives in white on wedding days. Some say that if bees make their nests in the roof of a house, none of the daughters will marry.

All beekeepers know not to go anywhere near their bees when the weather is bad, and that the threat of a storm will cause their bees to be grumpy and defensive. An old English proverb says that:

'When bees to distance wing their flight,
Days are warm and skies are bright.
But when their flight ends near their home,
Stormy weather is sure to come.'

It makes sense, of course, for bees to remain close to the hive if rain is about to fall, lest the falling water soaks their wings and washes them from the sky. Similarly a hive will only swarm is the colony is confident that the weather is settled and dry, and likely to remain so. The bees predict the weather in no mystical way but by detecting the pressure of the air. As high pressure decreases, and low pressure and bad weather comes in behind it, so the density of the air decreases and the humidity builds up. Low pressure makes the air thinner and flying harder work. Increased humidity leads to moisture on the wings of the bees and so increases their weight. Time to return to the hive. High pressure and the good weather that comes with it holds down scents close to the flowers that produce them and so make it easier for the bees to find forage.

Bees have often been regarded as wise and even holy insects, having foreknowledge as well as knowledge of many secret matters. In antiquity they were sometimes divine messengers, and their constant humming was believed to be a hymn of praise. Because of their status it is still considered unlucky in some places to kill a bee. If a bee flies into the house it is a sign of great good luck, or of the arrival of a stranger; however, the luck will only hold if the bee is allowed to either stay or to fly out of the house of its own accord. A bee landing on someone's hand is believed to foretell money to come, while if the bee settles on someone's head it means that person will rise to greatness. Bees were once considered to deliberately sting those who swore in front of them, and also to attack an adulterer or unchaste person; it was once held to be a sure sign that a girl was a virgin if she could walk through a swarm of bees without being stung.

An old English country tradition states that bees should not be purchased for money, as bought bees will never prosper. It was acceptable to barter goods of the same value in exchange for bees, and in some districts gold was an acceptable form of payment. A borrowed swarm or one given freely was more likely to do well; a stock of bees was often started from a borrowed swarm on the understanding that it would be returned if the giver was ever in need of it.

It is in theory not legal to buy and sell bees in England, though many do. In English law bees are *ferae naturae*, wild creatures in the care or keeping of the beekeeper. This may account for the many traditions associated with the buying and selling of bees. In Britain and in France it has long been considered unlucky to buy bees, though there is a long tradition of barter. And there are stories told of money being exchanged for bees out of sight of the bees themselves lest they swarm and leave their new keeper.

Not so in the USA where bees, being a valuable commodity when first brought to the New World, are legally chattels - movable property - and can be bought and sold with no worries about ill luck attending those involved.

Tanging the bees - making lots of noise when bees are swarming - seems to have had two functions. One was to alert neighbours that bees were swarming and to announce loudly that the person doing the tanging was the owner of the bees. Similarly the tanging could be used to make a claim on a found swarm. The other purpose was to encourage the bees to make a home in a new hive. Tanging is not a lost art. There are stories of its being done even today, with so much noise being made that a swarm of bees will settle at once and be able to be gathered up and hived before having the chance to fly far from their hive.

Some young birds come along, flying a yard or two at a time and lighting. Jim said it was a sign it was going to rain. He said it was a sign when young chickens flew that way, and so he reckoned it was the same way when young birds done it. I was going to catch some of them, but Jim wouldn't let me. He said it was death. He said his father laid mighty sick once, and some of them catched a bird, and his old granny said his father would die, and he did.

And Jim said you mustn't count the things you are going to cook for dinner, because that would bring bad luck. The same if you shook the table-cloth after sundown. And he said if a man owned a beehive and that man died, the bees must be told about it before sun-up next morning, or else the bees would all weaken down and quit work and die. Jim said bees wouldn't sting idiots; but I didn't believe that, because I had tried them lots of times myself, and they wouldn't sting me.

I had heard about some of these things before, but not all of them. Jim knowed all kinds of signs. He said he knowed most everything. I said it looked to me like all the signs was about bad luck, and so I asked him if there warn't any good-luck signs. He says: "Mighty few -- an' DEY ain't no use to a body. What you want to know when good luck's a-comin' for? Want to keep it off?"

Mark Twain, Huckleberry Finn

CANDLES AND WAXEN IMAGES

'The bee is the only creature which has come to us unchanged from Paradise and she gathers the wax for sacred services.'
German proverb

It is not easy to light a church, let alone a cathedral, if you have no gas or electricity. From the time they were first built, to special occasions today, the great religious buildings of the world have been lit by candle light. And the candles have been made of beeswax. Hence the long association between beekeeping and religious buildings, with monks famed as beekeepers even today. There is a Welsh tradition that bees came from Paradise, leaving the garden of Eden with Adam and Eve, but with the blessing of God so that man would have wax for the celebration of mass. 'The origin of bees is from Paradise, and for the sin of man they came thence, and God bestowed His blessing upon them; and for that reason the service of the mass cannot be performed without lighted tapers made of their wax.' So said Gwallter Machain, writing for the Fenni Eisteddfod in 1845. A German tradition echoes this, with a belief that the bee is the only creature to have come unchanged direct from Paradise.

In Christian churches, Jewish synagogues and Buddhist temples, candles are lit with a perpetual flame, a sign of the presence of the divine on earth. The first candles were made around 400 BC. None were used in homes until the 14th century and from then until the 19th century and the advent of paraffin, domestic candles were made from tallow - animal fat. Tallow candles were smelly and smoky and often gave off so much smoke that they obscured their own light. They dripped and what light they gave off was often feeble. Churches lit by tallow candles would become grimy with smoke and soot and filled with a gloomy smog. So for the Christian church especially, candles would be made of beeswax. The magic of beeswax was that it burnt with a clear light, was smoke free, and smelt divine. Hence the association between bees and purity. The burning of a beeswax candle was evidence enough of the purity of the wax and the bees that made it.

Candles were made by travelling chandlers, going from door to door and using the tallow or wax of the client to dip their wicks in and make the candles. The wax chandlers did not just dip candles, but traded in beeswax and all manner of beeswax products including torches, images, wax for seals, wax tablets for writing on and wax for medical uses. As cathedrals got bigger and the ceremonies inside them more elaborate, so the candles had to get bigger. Chandlers got together to protect their interests in fraternities and eventually the fraternities came together to form themselves into a guild - The Wax Chandlers Company. Today the Wax Chandlers Company is one of the City of London livery companies. In 1371 the Company gained control over the trade of Wax Chandlers in the City of London and in 1484 was granted a royal charter by Richard III. So it was that the wax chandlers lit the churches and cathedrals of England until the 1820s when the first candle making machines were invented and soon after paraffin was manufactured.

The chandlers often had links with other livery companies. In Paris the wax chandlers were one of four trades grouped in the *Epiciers-Apothecaires*: Spicers, Apothecaries, Wax Chandlers and Confectioners. What linked all four trades was the bee, since wax and honey were used then as today in all four trades.

But while beeswax candles may have held back the darkness and kept light in the world when the sun dipped over the horizon, there has always been a darker side to the uses of beeswax.

Icarus, the son of Daedalus, flew too near the sun on wings of feathers and wax. Daedalus was a skilled craftsman, and built for King Minos of Crete the Labyrinth from which none could escape. Fearful that Daedalus would tell of the Labyrinth's secret he had him imprisoned in a tower. The ingenious craftsman made two pairs of wings by sticking feathers to a wooden frame with beeswax. One pair he took for himself and the other pair he gave to his son, warning him that flying too close to the sun would cause the wax to melt. Giddy with the joys of flight, Icarus forgot his father's warning, the wax melted, the feathers came away and the boy plunged to his death in the sea.

Never was the dark side of a beeswax ritual shown more clearly than in the school rooms of Eton College in 1917. There the young Eric Blair became fascinated by stories of voodoo and the waxen effigies that could be used to cause pain and even death when moulded to the shape of the intended victim. One of the stories Blair read was 'The Leech of Folkestone', from 'The Ingoldsby Legends' which told of a maid who made a waxen image of her mistress and skewered it with a pin. The effect was deadly. Blair was being bullied by another boy at the school, Philip Yorke. With his friend Steven Runciman, Blair made a wax effigy of the bully. Years later Runicman recalled: 'Our making a wax effigy was, I am ashamed to say, my idea. Blair found that interesting and willingly collaborated. It was he who moulded the melted candle into a very crude human body. He wanted to stick a pin into the heart of our image, but that frightened me, so we compromised by breaking off his right leg, bent the leg of the model and pinched and pummelled it.' Blair was never bullied again. Yorke broke his leg a few days later, developed leukaemia and was dead within three months. So scared was Blair of what he had done, that he changed his name lest his enemies use his real name in magic against him. Eric Blair became George Orwell.

The making of voodoo dolls and their use in ritual and black magic is found in the slave population in Louisiana during the 18th and 19th centuries, where it arrived on the slave ships from west Africa. Then as now they are often known as poppets and are made of wax, adorned with beads, signs and symbols, and, if it can be obtained, the hair or nail clippings of the person the poppet represents.

It was not just amongst the African slaves that wax poppets were used to cause death and mischief. One was used in a plot against Pharoah Ramses III in ancient

Egypt. In renaissance Italy Galeazzo Visconti, the Duke of Milan, was accused of attempting to murder Pope John VIII with a wax doll. And in nineteenth century England, Caroline of Brunswick, the Princess of Wales, had a wax doll of her husband, the future King George IV, which she jabbed with pins.

The Duchess of Gloucester and Jane Shore were accused of using witchcraft in a plot against King Henry VI to enable Edward Duke of Gloucester to take the throne. In his telling of the story, Shakespeare has the Duchess of Gloucester ask the dishonest priest John Hume:

'What say'st thou, man? hast them as yet conferr'd
With Margery Jourdain, the cunning witch,
With Roger Bolingbroke, the conjurer?
And will they undertake to do me good?'

At her trial it was said that, 'there was found in the possession of herself and accomplices a waxen image of the king, which they melted in a magical manner before a slow fire, with the intention of making Henry's force and vigor waste away by like insensible degrees.'

When Edward's brother becomes King Richard III he rails against those who says have plotted against him, including Edward's wife Elizabeth, and used waxen images to twist his body into unnatural shapes:

'I pray you all, tell me what they deserve
That do conspire my death with devilish plots
Of damned witchcraft, and that have prevail'd
Upon my body with their hellish charms?
Look how I am bewitch'd; behold mine arm
Is, like a blasted sapling, wither'd up:
And this is Edward's wife, that monstrous witch,
Consorted with that harlot, strumpet Shore,
That by their witchcraft thus have marked me.'

This was the King who gave a Royal Charter to the Wax Chandlers.

When a wax doll of Queen Elizabeth I was found with a pin through its heart the Privy Council called in the necromancer John Dee to protect the Queen from the spell.

To some others at these times the Devil teaches how to make pictures of wax or clay. That by the roasting thereof, the persons that they bear the name of, may be continually melted or die away by continual sickness. They can bewitch and take the life of men or women, by roasting of the pictures, as I spoke of before, which likewise is very possible to their Master to perform, for although, as I said before, that instrument of wax has no virtue in that turn doing, yet may he not very well, even by the same measure that his conjured slaves, melts that wax in fire, may he not. I say at these times, subtly, as a spirit, so weaken and scatter the spirits of life of the patient, as may make him on the one part, for faintnesses, so sweat out the humour of his body. And on the other part, for the not concurrence of these spirits, which causes his digestion, so debilitate his stomach, that this humour redicall continually sweating out on the one part, and no new good sucks being put in the place thereof, for lack of digestion on the other, he shall at last vanish away, even as his picture will die in the fire.

King James I, Daemonologie

BEES, THE FINAL FRONTIER

What I am about to tell you is beyond belief, but let me assure you, every word is true.
Dr. John H. Watson, Sherlock Holmes in the 22nd Century

We are as curious about bees and wax and honey as ever we were. Health food shops are full of bee hive products, pollen and royal jelly, monofloral honeys, propolis, lotions and potions and unguents. Our belief in the power of honey and the things that come from the hive are as strong today as they were in times gone by. There is a continuity in myth, superstition and folklore that goes back to the very beginnings of recorded time, and stretches across continents and cultures. Only in Antarctica are no bees to be found and even there in the cold icy windswept spaces, explorers take bee based products to make their lives more comfortable.

In 1981 an amazingly well-preserved body was found at St Bees Priory in Cumbria. It was the body of a knight that had been wrapped in shrouds over which a wax-and-honey mixture had been poured. While the bodies around it had decomposed and were nothing more than skeletons, this body had survived for seven hundred years as if untouched by time. When the knight's body was unwrapped, he was found to be naked except for two pieces of string, one around his neck, the other around his penis. 'The pink hue of the skin quickly faded but the eyes were well preserved and the heart and intestines intact. The liver, when cut, appeared bright pink initially, and the vessels in other organs appeared to contain 'fresh' blood.'

Perhaps the greatest fictional beekeeper was Conan Doyle's Sherlock Holmes. When the great detective retired from London to Sussex at the beginning of the twentieth century he kept himself active as an apiarist:

'But you had retired, Holmes [says Dr Watson]. We heard of you as living the life of a hermit among your bees and your books in a small farm upon the South Downs.'

'Exactly, Watson. Here is the fruit of my leisured ease, the magnum opus of my latter years.' He picked up the volume from the table and read out the whole title, *Practical Handbook of Bee Culture, with some Observations upon the Segregation of the Queen*. 'Alone I did it. Behold the fruit of pensive nights and laborious days, when I watched the little working gangs as once I watched the criminal world of London.'

The children's animated television series 'Sherlock Holmes in the 22nd Century', tells how on his death, Holmes' corpse was preserved in a glass-walled, honey filled coffin in the basement of Scotland Yard. Two hundred years after his death, Holmes' body is rejuvenated by biologist Sir Evan Hargreaves to combat a clone of the original criminal mastermind Professor Moriarty.

While the rejuvenation of honey embalmed corpses remains a thing for the future, today medical research continues to validate many of the claims made for honey. England's National Health Service has beekeepers who produce honey products especially for medical use. As I was writing this book, a story appeared in London's 'Daily Mail' newspaper of a man who had a near miraculous cure of an eye condition from the application of some honey:

A man who spent eight years searching for a cure for a chronic eye condition was amazed when he finally found the remedy in a 99p jar of Tesco Value honey.

Frank Dougan, 62, lost his left eye when he was shot with a bow and arrow in a childhood accident and he later developed a painful infection called blepharitis.

He visited doctors and eye specialists and spent a fortune on different drops over the years but nothing worked.

But he was finally cured when he cut his hand while on holiday in Jerusalem and he was advised to put honey on it.

Surprised by the results, when he returned home to Glasgow he bought a jar of Tesco Value Honey and tried it on his eyelid - and within weeks the infection had cleared.

He said yesterday: 'It's unbelievable. It's incredibly effective. I have spent a fortune on prescription eye drops over the years, I have a fridge full of them.

'It's funny that at the end of it all the cure would come in the form of a 99p jar of honey from the supermarket. And it's not bad on toast either.' (Daily Mail, 25 July 2012)

I was checking a hive on the roof of the clothing company Ted Baker, when a new member of staff got chatting to me. He was from Hungary and knew something about beekeeping. Had I ever been stung, he asked. Of course, I answered. Then you must be very strong sexually he told me. How so, I asked? 'In my country,' he told me, 'we deliberately get stung to improve out virility.' I thought back on the stories in this book, and on Richard Burton's tales of the aphrodisiac uses of honey. 'I'll stick to honey on toast rather than getting deliberately stung,' I told him, 'it seems to work for me.'

Thanks and acknowledgements are due to:

My friends and fellow beekeepers Helen Jukes and Liz Turner for advice on the manuscript; Andre Lemmer for introducing me to the story of the Mantis and the Bee; Jeremy Burbidge of Northern Bee Books for his encouragement and support; David Miller for his design; and to Marco Toro for his delightful lino-cuts.

'What is not good for the swarm is not good for the bee.'
Marcus Aurelius

INDEX

Aeneas 27
Aesop 29
Afghanistan 8
Africa 1, 7-9
Amaltheia 12
America 33, 37
ambrosia 14-17
Ancient Greeks 1, 11, 15, 17
aphrodisiac 17, 19
Arabia 1
arthritis 22
ayurvedic medicine 18

Bielobog 4
Bible 18
birthday cake 1

Bulgaria 5
Burton, Isabel 22
Burton, Sir Richard 19-20, 22, 47
Bushman 3, 7, 12, 15

Cartland, Dame Barbara 15
Chernobog 4
Cherokee 33

Devil 5, 43
Dionysus 13

elephant 4-5, 8-9
embalming 23, 45-46
Friar Tuck 9

hedgehog 5
Hindus 17
Homer 25-26
honey badger 7-8
honeymoon 1, 19
Honeyguide bird 7-8
Hungary 47

Icarus 40-41
Ireland 31-33, 35

Japan 35
Judaism 18, 39

Kouretes 11-12
Kundalini 17-18

Leonardo da Vinci 14

Mantis 3
Manuka honey 22-23
mead 1, 12, 18
Melissa 11-12
Middle East 5

nectar 14-16
New Zealand 22
Norse myths 18
nymphs 11-12

Odysseus 16, 25-27
Orwell, George 41
Ovid 13

Penelope 26-27
Perfumed Garden 19-21

rheumatism 22

saints 28, 31-35
San 3, 8, 12
Shakespeare 42
Sherlock Holmes 45, 46
Song of Solomon 6
Switzerland 35

tanging 12, 37
Ted Baker 47
Tesco 46-47
Thailand 4
Titans 11, 13-14
Twain, Mark 38

Virgil 27-28

Wax Chandlers Company 40, 42

Zeus 11-14, 16-17, 24-25, 29

'It is dearly bought honey, that is licked off a thorn.'
French proverb